BRITISH RAILWAYS

PAST and PRESENT

No 15

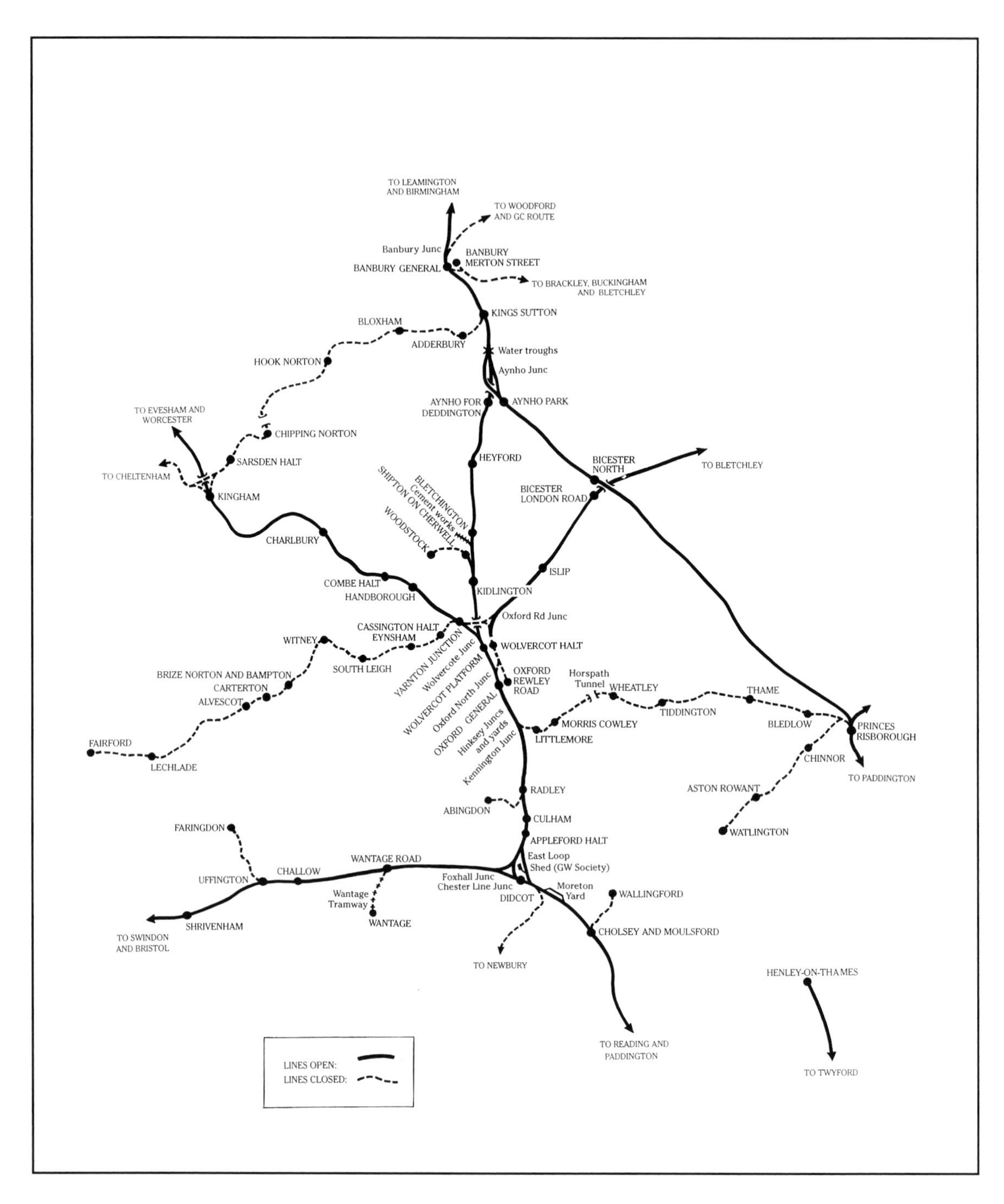

BRITISH RAILWAYS PAST & PRESENT No 15: OXFORDSHIRE - This book presents a detailed examination of the changing face of the railways in the region depicted in this map, which includes locations featured in the photographs or mentioned in the text. The pictures have been chosen to provide a balanced view, including railways which are still in use or being developed, together with scenes where the lines have been closed and either abandoned or redeveloped since the 'past' pictures were taken.

PAST and PRESENT

No 15

Oxfordshire

Laurence Waters & Tony Doyle

Past and Present

Past & Present Publishing Ltd

CHARLBURY is one of Oxfordshire's most attractive and distinctive surviving stations. On the left of this 1920s view is the coal yard of James Marriot, and on the right Charlbury Gas Works which opened in the 1880s and closed on 31 March 1951. The sidings in the foreground were removed in 1968 when the platform was extended.

With the rationalisation of the 'Cotswold line' (see pages 106ff) in 1971 the track was singled and the down platform removed, but luckily the up station building was retained and refurbished. Looking down from the same spot in March 1992 the extent of the rationalisation can be clearly seen. *Authors' Collection/AD*

CONTENTS

First published in 1992
Reprinted 1994
Reprinted 2004

British Library Cataloguing in Publication Data

A catalogue record for this book is available from the British Library

ISBN 1 85895 059 7

Past & Present Publishing Ltd
The Trundle
Ringstead Road
Great Addington
Kettering
Northants
NN14 4BW

Tel/Fax: 01536 330588
email: sales@nostalgiacollection.com
Website: www.nostalgiacollection.com

Maps drawn by Christina Siviter

Printed and bound in Great Britain

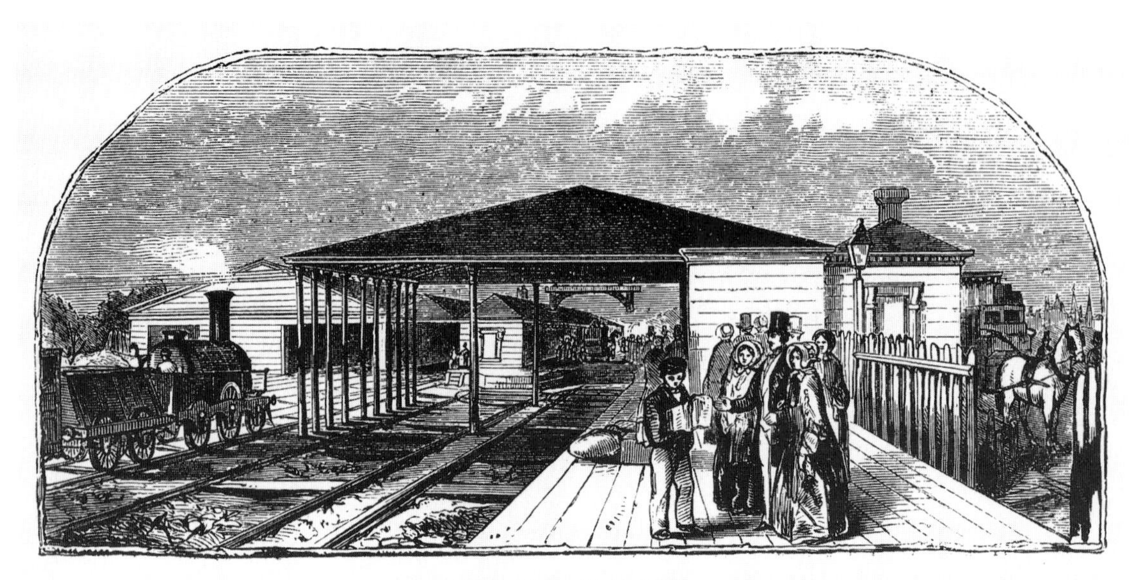

OXFORD STATION.

OXFORD: The ultimate past and present combination? This Measom lithograph shows the original Oxford Station at Granpont in 1852, the year that it was closed to passenger traffic; it had been opened by the Oxford Railway Company in June 1844. Looking at early track plans this drawing is quite an accurate representation of the station. On the left is the large goods shed and on the right the station road and the spires of Oxford. The station remained open for goods traffic until 26 November 1872 (the date of the removal of the broad gauge at Oxford); the site then remained derelict for a number of years before being used for the construction of new housing.

This is the old station site today. The road on the left is Western Road and was the road leading to the old station. It was named Western Road in around 1882, long after the old station had been closed. In the foreground is Marlborough Road which was built on the trackbed of the old line. *Authors' Collection/LW*

INTRODUCTION

The Great Western Railway first entered Oxfordshire in June 1840 when the Reading to Steventon section of Brunel's main line from London to Bristol bisected the county boundary to the east of Goring. The City of Oxford was connected to the rail network in June 1844 with the opening by the Oxford Railway Company of a 9½-mile branch from Didcot Junction. Prior to this passengers from Oxford had to travel south and use the station at Steventon. The construction of the Oxford Railway and its subsequent extension through to Birmingham in 1852 gave the Great Western, and Brunel in particular, a Broad Gauge foothold in the Midlands.

By the turn of the century the railway map in the county was almost complete, with very few Oxfordshire towns and villages more than a few miles from a station. And by then it was not just the Great Western that dominated the county because the London & North Western Railway had its own lines serving both Oxford and Banbury.

The growth of lines in Oxfordshire essentially came to an end in April 1910 with the completion by the Great Western of the 18¼-mile Ashendon Junction to Ayhno section of the Paddington to Birmingham 'cut off' route.

A general increase in passenger traffic between the two wars saw the Great Western open several new passenger Halts in the county, and during the Second World War the railway network was expanded once again with new goods yards being opened at Yarnton, Banbury, Hinksey and Moreton (Didcot). The resulting increase in traffic both during and after the war meant that Oxford became an operating bottleneck, a situation that continued for many years.

During the 1950s the county saw its first branch line closures with Faringdon, Woodstock, Wallingford and Watlington all losing their passenger services. By 1963 they had been joined by Chipping Norton, Thame, Fairford and Abingdon.

Steam traction came to an end in the county during September 1966. The very last official Western Region steam working had taken place several months earlier when, on 3 January 1966, No 6998 *Burton Agnes Hall* pulled the 2.20 pm service from Bournemouth to York between Oxford and Banbury.

It is interesting to reflect that in 1950 there were 64 stations open in Oxfordshire, while today there are just 22. For such a small county Oxford was blessed with a wide variety of lines and although many of these are now closed the area still continues to provide many interesting locations for the railway photographer.

In 1974 new boundary changes saw Didcot and much of the Vale of the White Horse, previously in Berkshire, absorbed into Oxfordshire. Therefore, in order to make matters simple and the book more interesting, we have decided to use the 'new' Oxfordshire as our boundary line. This has enabled us to include many of these locations, to the south of Oxford, that would have otherwise been excluded.

In selecting the pictures we have resisted the temptation to include a train in every shot. We both feel that, certainly at some locations, the inclusion of a train often obscures much of the interesting detail that was once there and has now gone.

Producing this book has certainly been great fun, albeit tinged with a certain amount of sadness, travelling around the county revisiting many of those long gone lines and stations. In conclusion we would like to thank the many photographers and organisations who have supplied the 'past' pictures.

Laurence F. Waters
Antony E. Doyle
Oxford

Postscript Since June 1992 all Network SouthEast loco-hauled services between Oxford and Paddington have been replaced by the new Network Class '165' Turbo units.

West of Didcot

SHRIVENHAM: An unidentified 'Castle' hurries through Shrivenham with a Bristol-Paddington service in the early 1960s. Shrivenham station was opened on 17 December 1840 when the Great Western main line from Paddington was extended through to Wootton Bassett Road. The station building is typical of that period; note the large ex-Broad Gauge goods shed.

Shrivenham station was closed on 7 December 1964. On 2 March 1992 only the platform faces remain as an HST rushes through on a Swansea to Paddington service. *GW Trust/LW*

UFFINGTON was opened on 1 June 1864 and was the junction station for the branch line to Faringdon. A feature here was the large girder roadbridge, erected in 1897 and replacing a level crossing. In the 'past' picture, taken on 16 May 1959, 'Hall' No 5978 *Bodinnick Hall* runs in with an up stopping service. The signal box was opened in 1897 and closed on 3 March 1968.

Like Shrivenham, Uffington was closed to passenger traffic on 7 December 1964. The large girder bridge still marks the site today, and a signalling relay building now stands on the spot once occupied by Uffington Signal Box. *M. Hale/LW*

Faringdon branch

FARINGDON: The $3^{1}/_{2}$-mile Faringdon Railway was opened on 1 June 1864. There were no intermediate stations on the branch, which terminated in the small market town. The first view, taken in 1919, shows the single-platform terminus station (centre), the engine shed (left) and the goods depot (right). The branch closed to passengers on 31 December 1951 but remained open for goods traffic until 1 July 1963.

Like many other closed stations the area has now become an industrial estate, but the roof of the station can just be seen in the second picture, taken from the estate access road in March 1992.

The building, which is listed, is now used as a coffee/antique shop, as can be seen from the third view. *Authors' Collection/LW*

CHALLOW

CHALLOW: The first picture shows the picturesque station at Challow (Faringdon Road until 1 June 1864) in 1919. During 1932 the Great Western undertook many improvements to the main line through the Vale of the White Horse, and the view above, dated 8 April 1932, shows reconstruction work in progress. The two-track layout was widened to four and the platforms were lengthened.

Like all the other stations in the Vale, Challow was closed on 7 December 1964, and today (left) the track is once again double, and only the platform faces remain. *GW Trust/LW*

WANTAGE ROAD station looking west. In true Great Western fashion the station was situated some 2 miles from the town of Wantage. The first picture was taken around the turn of the century and shows the original two-track layout.

The second photograph was taken in the 1950s and shows the new four-track layout and the rebuilt station.

The station was, again, closed on 7 December 1964, and the third picture, taken on 2 March 1992, shows that only the overgrown platform faces now mark the spot. *Authors' Collection/LW*

Wantage Tramway

THE WANTAGE TRAMWAY was opened 11 October 1875; it ran from the goods yard at Wantage Road station and along the Wantage Road for 2 miles to a small terminus station. For the first year or so the tramway was operated by horse, but a regular steam service commenced from 1 August 1876. The tramway closed to passengers on 1 August 1925 and to goods on 19 December 1945. In the first picture, taken in around 1905, Hughes tram engine No 3 with cars 1 and 3 pose for the photographer at Lockinge Park, just south of Wantage Road station. The incline up to the road bridge over the main line can just be seen in the background.

Looking at the second picture, taken on 2 March 1992, it seems hard to believe that it all ever happened. The distant road bridge is the only reference point. *Authors' Collection/LW*

STEVENTON station was opened on 1 June 1840 and immediately became the main railhead for Oxford; in fact, the Great Western was at one time going to name it Oxford Road. The station's importance at this time is well illustrated by the fact that in 1842 alone some 77,000 passengers and 12,500 tons of goods were dealt with. The impressive station superintendent's house, seen in the top right-hand corner of both pictures, was used between 21 July 1842 and 5 January 1843 for Great Western company board meetings. The first picture was taken looking west from the old A34 roadbridge on 26 May 1962. The station was once again one of those closed on 7 December 1964, and the goods shed was removed in May 1965.

Today the station is just a memory, its location identified by milepost 56½ and, of course, the fine Great Western buildings. *M. Hale/LW*

MILTON: At 1.13 pm on 22 November 1955 a Treherbert to Paddington excursion hauled by 'Britannia' No 70026 *Polar Star* was derailed at speed at Milton. The engine together with several of the coaches rolled down the embankment, making retrieval difficult. The engine had to eventually be removed by building a special track from the nearby ordnance depot. The picture of No 70026, taken on 28 November, shows the rather unfortunate locomotive at the bottom of the embankment.

The whole area today forms part of the new Milton trading estate, but the exact position can be marked by milepost $55\frac{1}{4}$ which can just be glimpsed at the upper left of the photograph. *Authors' Collection/LW*

Didcot

FOXHALL JUNCTION, pictured here on 15 August 1965, was opened on 15 February 1886 when the new West loop round to the Oxford line was constructed. The signal box seen was a replacement for an earlier box and was opened on 13 October 1931; it was closed on 17 May 1965. The large building in the background is the old GW horse provender store.

A new road bridge has afforded the 'present' view of the junction, which today is controlled from the power box at Reading. *M. Hale/LW*

DIDCOT (1): 'Castle' No 5040 *Stokesay Castle* approaches Didcot with the 2.55 pm stopping service from Swindon on 4 September 1961; the engine is on an ex-works running-in turn. The large wooden shed behind the shed is the old broad/standard gauge transfer shed.

The same location but from a slightly higher viewpoint shows another 'Castle', this time Class '47' No 47835 *Windsor Castle,* arriving with a Bristol-Paddington service. The large provender store was demolished in April 1976 and during 1979 the transfer shed was itself 'transferred' to the nearby Didcot Railway Centre. Out of sight in the older view but visible in the centre background of the 1990 one is the recently demolished provender store superintendent's house. *W. Turner/LW*

DIDCOT (2): The Great Western, under the auspices of the Oxford Railway Company, opened its branch from Didcot to Oxford on 12 June 1844, and Didcot was placed on the railway map for the first time with the opening of Didcot Junction station, pictured here in the early 1920s. Note the Station Master's house on the right.

The scene today has altered somewhat. The old station frontage has been swept away and replaced by the modern structure pictured here. Didcot Parkway, as it is now known, was opened on 29 July 1985. The new entrance building contains a ticket office, snack bar and parcels office, although the travel centre has since closed. *Authors' Collection/LW*

CHESTER LINE JUNCTION pictured in 1906, showing to good effect the original track layout. On the extreme left is the down main; the line curving into it is the down relief. The up main passes through the centre the picture from top left to bottom right. In the centre is Didcot West End signal box, and to the right the large horse provender store built in 1884. In 1934 the station was enlarged and at the same time the track layout was improved.

Looking from approximately the same vantage point, a pair of Class '37s' stand in the yard. On the left is the new footbridge to the Parkway car park and on the right Didcot Power Station, completed in 1971. *Authors' Collection/LW*

DIDCOT (3): In this 1950s shot 0-6-0 No 3211 runs through platform 3 at Didcot with a local goods service from the Newbury line.

Today the new footbridge (see previous page) offers the photographer a better view of what is essentially the same location, as No 6998 *Burton Agnes Hall* departs on Saturday 29 February 1992 with a Network SouthEast steam special to Oxford, being run in connection with the Cholsey station centenary. In the background No 71000 *Duke of Gloucester* stands at the old Eynsham platform in the Didcot Railway Centre. *R. H. G. Simpson/LW*

DIDCOT (4): This excellent shot, taken on 21 April 1956, shows ex-LSWR 'T9' 4-4-0 No 30285 waiting at Didcot with the afternoon service to Southampton via the Didcot, Newbury & Southampton line. In the background 0-6-0 No 2209 passes by on the east loop with an Oxford line freight.

The use of No 6998 on the steam specials of 29 February 1992 enabled us to partially recreate the above shot as Class '47' No 47822 rushes past with the Glasgow Central-Poole service. *R. C. Riley/LW*

DIDCOT SHED YARD, pictured in April 1960, was host to No 4959 *Purley Hall* and '9F' 2-10-0 No 92002. The engine shed at Didcot was opened in June 1932, replacing an earlier shed that stood adjacent to the station. It was closed to steam traction on 14 June 1965, although it continued to be used as a diesel stabling point until 1969.

During 1966 the Great Western Society moved its first items of rolling-stock into the engine shed and in September 1969 Didcot Railway Centre was established. We think that you will agree that this is one set of pictures where the now is definitely better than the then! From left to right are Nos 5572, 6106, 7808 *Cookham Manor*, 5051 *Drysllwyn Castle* and 3822. *Both LW*

MORETON YARD, a couple of miles to the east of Didcot, was opened in March 1941. In this picture, taken on 22 September 1961, ex-WD 2-8-0 No 90565 leaves the yard with an up goods. The yard closed in 1964 and was lifted soon afterwards.

The entrance still can be clearly seen on 3 April 1992 as an HST speeds by with a Bristol-Paddington service. *M. Mensing/LW*

Wallingford branch

The Wallingford branch was opened by the Wallingford & Watlington Railway Company on 2 July 1866. The $3^1/_2$-mile branch (it was never extended through to Watlington) joined the main line at Wallingford Road station (Moulsford). On 29 February 1892 Wallingford Road was closed and a new station was opened approximately 1 mile further west at Cholsey and from that date Wallingford branch services ran into a bay platform at the new station. Passenger services were withdrawn on 15 June 1959 and goods services on 13 September 1965, although the line remained open as a long siding in order to serve the large ABM plant. In 1969 the station site at Wallingford was sold to a local builder. Today, what remains of the branch is being operated by the Cholsey & Wallingford Railway Preservation Society.

WALLINGFORD: The first picture (*above left*) shows Wallingford station in the 1930s. The small coaling stage and engine shed can be seen on the left, while some youthful spotters stand by the cattle pens.

In the second picture (*left*) Reading (81D)-allocated 0-4-2T No 1407 waits at the platform on 6 March 1959. By this date the small engine shed had been closed and the track lifted.

In the final picture (*above*), taken in October 1991, an entrance road to a housing estate covers the area of the station. The main reference point on all three pictures is the wooden-gabled house in the centre, but notice how the conifer, seen on the left behind the water crane ladder in the 1959 picture, has grown in the ensuing years. *Authors' Collection/J. D. Edwards/LW*

Henley-on-Thames

The 4 1/2-mile branch from Twyford to Henley-on-Thames was opened by the GWR on 1 July 1857. Initially the only intermediate station was at Shiplake, where the River Thames was crossed via a timber viaduct, but a second station at Wargrave was opened in 1900. The branch was doubled in 1896, but singled once again in 1961. In 1975 the overall roof at Henley, together with the station building, was removed, but the 1904 platform canopy was retained. During the 1980s the station was completely rebuilt with a new entrance building and a single platform.

HENLEY-ON-THAMES: The first picture (*above left*), taken from around the turn of the century, shows to good effect the original station entrance and the large overall roof behind it.

On 10 May 1992 much of the forecourt area has been sold and redeveloped, so it is now impossible to attain the same angle. We have therefore included the following two pictures to show both the new station entrance (*left*) and the single platform layout (*above*), still covered by the 1904 canopy. *BR/LW/LW*

Watlington branch

The $8^{1}/_{2}$-mile Watlington & Princes Risborough Railway was opened on 15 August 1872. The line ran alongside the Chiltern Hills to terminate at the small market town of Watlington. Passenger services were withdrawn on 1 July 1957 but the line remained open for the weekly coal service from Toton to Chinnor Cement Works until 1990. At the time of writing a preservation society has been formed to try to save and operate this remaining section of line.

CHINNOR: The stone-built station is pictured shortly after its closure to passenger traffic (*above*). The station building was used for a while after closure as a mess room for loco crews shunting the cement works sidings.

By 1991 the station is no more, but the terraced houses on the left have been extended and converted into offices. *J. D. Edwards/LW*

ASTON ROWANT (1): Ex-GWR 0-6-0 No 3697 with auto-trailer No W181 arrives at Aston Rowant with the 2.32 pm service from Princes Risborough on 8 September 1956. Aston Rowant, like many other rural stations, was situated some way from the village.

The site today is used as a storage site by the county council. The Chiltern Hills in the distance identify the spot, although part of the station railings could just be seen on the right. *H. Ballantyne/LW*

ASTON ROWANT (2): Another shot of the station looking towards Watlington. Notice how the rails dip under the roadbridge which carried the Stokenchurch road over the tracks at this point. The ground frame hut controlled the single siding on the left.

The second picture shows how sometimes the railway can disappear for ever. It was taken from roadbridge seen in the 'past' picture and again looks in the Watlington direction. The bridge still remains but has now been filled in - its brick abutments can just be seen in the centre. The cutting, however, has been completely ploughed over. *H. Ballantyne/LW*

WATLINGTON: The 2.50 pm service from Princes Risborough, hauled by 0-6-0PT No 4680, arrives at Watlington on 11 June 1957. The station yard contained a small goods shed and a carriage shed, the latter being the structure on the right. There was also a wooden engine shed here but this was burned down in 1906 and not replaced.

The station, carriage shed and goods shed still survive today as part of the Shirburn Castle estate, and all are in remarkably good condition. The carriage shed is now used for storing farm machinery. *J. Bearpark/LW*

APPLEFORD HALT (1): Some locations never seem to change and one of these is Appleford Halt. The halt was opened on 11 September 1933 and is pictured here in the 1950s as 'Castle' No 4093 *Dunster Castle* runs through with a down Worcester service.

On 3 April 1992 Class '47' No 47314 speeds through with a Didcot-Bescot freight. During the last few years a certain amount of refurbishment work has taken place, including replacement of the platforms. *Both LW*

APPLEFORD HALT (2): Looking northwards from the down platform, again in the late 1950s, 2-6-2T No 6122 arrives with a stopping service from Oxford to Reading.

The same service 1992-style shows a two-car DMU arriving with the 12.48 pm service from Oxford to Reading. Note the relocation of the steps down to the up platform. *Both LW*

CULHAM: This delightful station is pictured here in 1919. It was opened on 12 June 1844, and prior to the opening of the Abingdon branch in 1856 it was named Abingdon Road. Note the ivy-covered signal box on the up platform and lovely Brunel-designed station building.

In March 1992, whilst much of the old station has gone, the Brunel building on the up platform is listed and is therefore safe, for the time being at least. The ex-Admiralty stores seen in the background are now used by the Ministry of Transport, but the bulk of the site now forms part of the Jet project (Joint European Taurus). *Authors' Collection/LW*

Abingdon branch

The Abingdon Branch was opened by the Abingdon Railway Company on 2 June 1856. It ran from a small interchange station, situated just north of the Nuneham river bridge on the main Didcot-Oxford line, to a single-platform terminus station at Abingdon. In September 1872 the branch was converted to standard gauge and on 8 September 1873 services were extended to the newly completed interchange station at Radley. Passenger services were withdrawn from Abingdon on 9 September 1963 and goods services on 30 June 1984.

ABINGDON (1): In the first picture (*above*), taken in the mid-1950s, a pair of Oxford Motor Services AEC double-deck buses await the arrival of the branch service from Radley.

Today only the platform face remains. The trackbed has become a car park and even the railway pub (centre right) is closed. *R. H. G. Simpson/LW*

VAN HOUTENS COCOA
VAN HOUTENS COCOA
ROYAL INSURANCE COMPANY
DALE, FORTY & Co's
Pianos
CHELTENHAM
TOWER TEA
TOWER TEA
G.W.R.
STONES Original GINGER WINE

ABINGDON (2): Amongst the hoardings seen here in 1903 on the original station at Abingdon (*top*) is a GWR poster advertising a special excursion to Birmingham to watch Aston Villa play Everton in the English First Division. This station was badly damaged in a shunting accident on 22 April 1908 and was subsequently replaced by the new station (*above*), seen in April 1910. This fine structure lasted for a number of years after the line was closed to passengers, but sadly was demolished in 1971. The third picture (*left*) shows the same site today - almost all of the old buildings are gone, but still standing at the time of writing are the old horse stables, the roof of which can just be seen to the right centre. *Authors' Collection (2)/LW*

ABINGDON (3): The daily goods service from Abingdon to Hinksey hauled by 0-4-2T No 1435 stands in the yard at Abingdon on 7 September 1961.

Goods services effectively ceased in 1980 when the MG car plant closed down. The local coal yard continued to be served as required, but in 1984 this also closed and so did the line. The large malthouse is the obvious reference point between the two pictures, but note also that some of the station fencing remains on 15 March 1992. *Tony Doyle/LW*

RADLEY (1): There were no intermediate stations between Abingdon and the interchange station at Radley. In this pre-First World War shot probably the whole of the station staff at Radley pose for the photographer. Note the normal width between the up and down lines, since Radley was constructed after the removal of the broad gauge.

The station today is an unstaffed halt, all of the original buildings having been removed, although what is left of the footbridge has recently been refurbished. This incidentally is now the only access to the up platform, hardly an ideal situation for the disabled! *Author's Collection/LW*

RADLEY (2): Abingdon branch services ran into the bay platform at Radley. Here, in 1952, 0-4-2T No 1425 awaits departure for Abingdon. The two sidings were used for stabling branch stock.

Today the old Abingdon platform remains but the trackbed (the track was removed in 1974) is now used as a car park. In this picture, taken in February 1992, passengers are definitely in the minority as a three-car 'Thames Line' DMU calls *en route* to Reading. Note that the roadbridge on the extreme left to Lower Radley has recently been rebuilt. *R. H. G. Simpson/LW*

RADLEY (3): Another shot, taken in 1955, shows to good advantage the overall layout at the station. The Abingdon branch sidings are to the right, whilst 2-6-2T No 6138 leaves the down platform with a local service from Didcot to Oxford.

Looking down from the same spot today, an unidentified Class '37' runs through with the Fawley to Longport LPG tanker train. *GW Trust/LW*

Oxford to Princes Risborough

The 'Risborough branch' was opened by the Wycombe Railway Company in two stages, first between Princes Risborough and Thame on 1 August 1862, then between Thame and Kennington Junction on 24 October 1864. Passenger services were withdrawn on 6 January 1963, but the line remained open for use until May 1967, after which the centre portion between Horspath and Thame was lifted.

KENNINGTON JUNCTION: The branch left the main line at Kennington Junction and crossed the Thames via a girder bridge. On 3 September 1959 (*above*) ex-GWR 2-8-0 No 3857 approaches the junction with a freight off the branch from the Morris Cowley yard.

Removal of the old semaphore signals and the height of the *Leylandii* trees in the foreground has now made it impossible to achieve the same viewpoint. Class '47' No 47362 runs off the branch on 11 March 1992 with the 15.00 4M15 service from Morris Cowley to Longbridge. *J. D. Edwards/LW*

LITTLEMORE: The first station on the branch after leaving Oxford was at Littlemore, seen here, looking east, at around the turn of the century. The large building on the right was the County Lunatic Asylum.

After passenger services were withdrawn the station building saw further light industrial use, but today what is left of it has been swallowed up within a small works. The line remains open to serve a nearby oil terminal together with the large freight terminal at Morris Cowley. The building on the right is now the Littlemore Psychiatric Hospital . . . *Authors' Collection/LW*

COWLEY: Engineering work over the cut-off route via Bicester saw the Risborough branch regularly used as a diversionary route. On 11 September 1960 'Hall' No 6934 *Beachamwell Hall* runs past the large Blackbird Leys housing estate at Cowley with the diverted 4.10 pm Paddington-Wolverhampton service.

In 1967 the line was closed beyond Horspath and today this section is open as far as the Cowley Freight Terminal. On 3 April 1992 Class '47' No 47050 passes the same spot with the 15.00 4M15 service from Cowley to Longbridge. This train is regularly loaded with up to 10 'cartics' (equivalent to 97 Standard Length Vehicles) and is nearly $^{1}/_{2}$ mile long! The siding on the left, seen in both pictures, once served the nearby car plant but, as can be seen, it is now unused. *M. Mensing/LW*

MORRIS COWLEY station was opened in 1928 to serve the nearby motor works, named after William Morris, the founder of Morris Motors Ltd. This was actually the second station on this site; the first, Garsington Bridge Halt, was opened on 1 February 1908 for the newly introduced railmotor services to Thame, but was closed on 22 March 1915 when the railmotor services were withdrawn. The station continued to be used for a number of years after closure by a car delivery firm before being 'accidently' burned to the ground.

The area today has changed somewhat. The steel overbridge was constructed in 1970 in order to ferry cars from the nearby Rover works over the line to the freight terminal where they are loaded on to the cartic wagons for distribution throughout this country and abroad. *Authors' Collection/LW*

HORSPATH (1): At Horspath the line ran via an embankment and a cutting into the 564-yard Horspath Tunnel. The first shot shows Class '47' No D1741 approaching Butts Road Bridge with a diverted Wolverhampton-Paddington service on 19 March 1967.

The second picture needs little comment other than that the overgrown trackbed here is popular for walking dogs! *S. Boorne/LW*

HORSPATH (2): Looking in the opposite direction the same train is seen approaching the tunnel entrance.

Once the trackbed was removed drainage in the cutting became almost non-existent and during a particularly wet period a major landslip occurred which resulting in a number of the houses built near the top of the cutting losing their back gardens down the slope. *S. Boorne/LW*

WHEATLEY: During the Second World War it could be argued that Wheatley became the most important station on the branch; this was because of its close proximity to the military hospital at Holton. During this time it was certainly the busiest with many special ambulance trains arriving at the station from where the casualties were transferred to the hospital by road.

In the picture above, 'Castle' No 5089 *Westminster Abbey* runs through the station on Sunday 11 September 1960 with the diverted 2.10 pm service from Paddington to Birkenhead.

As already mentioned, the stretch of line between Horspath and Thame was finally closed to all traffic on 1 May 1967. In 1969 the cutting to the west of Wheatley station together with the adjacent road bridge was filled in. The whole site including the adjacent Avery's woodyard has recently been cleared to make way for new housing (*right*) and soon the only evidence of a railway here will be The Railway pub! *M. Mensing/LW*

TIDDINGTON was situated approximately half way between Wheatley and Thame, and is seen here in the 1950s. The platform contained a single wooden station building, and a siding served a small cattle dock at the Oxford end of the station.

The site today is used by the County Council as a road depot. The only reference points between the two photographs are the remains of the trackbed and the large tree on the left, although the entrance to the station is still clearly visible from the main road. *Authors' Collection/LW*

THAME was the most important intermediate station on the branch. It was opened by the Wycombe Railway on 2 August 1862, and the Brunel-designed overall roof can clearly be seen as 2-6-2T No 6156 on the 10.00 am service from Oxford takes on water and receives attention to its fire on Sunday 4 February 1962.

The line from Princes Risborough to the oil terminal (seen under the bridge) remained open for deliveries by rail until the terminal closed during September 1991. For many years the station site had remained derelict, but in the late 1980s a new industrial estate was built in the old goods yard. At the time of writing the future of this section of the old Wycombe Railway remains uncertain. *B. Jennings/LW*

BLEDLOW, lying just over the border in Bucks, is seen here on 25 August 1962 as 2-6-2T No 6124 arrives with the 7.50 am service from Oxford. Note the small signal box and also the road crossing.

The station building still survives as a private residence with shrubs and flowers decorating the platform face in this picture taken on 2 March 1992. *Both LW*

Oxford

We return to the main Didcot-Oxford line just north of Kennington Junction, whose splitting homes can just be glimpsed in the background of this 1958 view, taken from the Redbridge, as ex-Southern Railway 'King Arthur' No 30771 ***Sir Sagramore*** approaches the southern outskirts of Oxford with a Bournemouth-York service.

During the 1960s the new southern ring road was completed, and the bridge carrying the road over the railway can be seen in the second shot as No 47620 ***Windsor Castle*** (now 47835) passes the same spot with the Poole-Newcastle service. *J. D. Edwards/LW*

HINKSEY SOUTH: 'Hall' No 5960 *St Edmund Hall* passes the signal box at Hinksey South on 24 June 1961 with a Saturday extra from Birmingham to Bournemouth. Hinksey South, which was constructed by a labour force of Italian POWs, was opened on 29 March 1942, and controlled the southern entrance to Hinksey Yard which was also completed during the same year.

The box closed on 18 December 1973. Looking from the same spot on 3 April 1992, we see Class '47' No 47636 *Sir John de Graeme* accelerating away from Oxford with the 14.00 Network service to Paddington. The rural-looking field on the right in the first shot is now occupied by Cliffords Dairies. *Dr G. Smith/LW*

HINKSEY NORTH: 'Grange' No 6841 *Marlas Grange* leaves Oxford in the early 1960s with a Saturday extra from the Midlands to the South Coast. From left to right are the northern entrance to Hinksey marshalling yards, Oxford Gasworks, and the then recently completed tower of Nuffield College.

In March 1992 Class '47' No 47579 *James Nightall GC* passes the same spot with the 10.00 am service to London. Today Hinksey yard is all but closed and the gasworks are only a memory, the flat skyline being broken by the girder structure of the new ice rink, the tower of Oxford Castle and, of course, that of Nuffield College. *R. H. G. Simpson/LW*

Oxford General (GWR)

GENERAL (1): This is the small goods yard at Becket Street, opened in about 1870 and pictured in around 1920. The cattle pens in the foreground were used to load and unload livestock for the local cattle market which was only a short distance away.

The yard fell out of use in the early 1970s and was used for a number of years as a motor vehicle scrapyard - a fine advert for passengers arriving at this most beautiful of cities! With the construction of the new station, the site has now been cleared and may possibly be used for a new multi-storey car park. *Authors' Collection/LW*

GENERAL (2): The Great Western station at Oxford is seen here from the Station South signal box (in the left background of the 'past' photo opposite) in about 1919. Oxford General was opened on 1 October 1852 and originally featured an overall roof, but this was removed during 1891 when the station was rebuilt. In 1910 the north end of the up platform was extended - the separate roof awning can be seen at centre left. The bridge in the foreground carries the railway over Botley Road.

In 1971 the old station was demolished and replaced by a temporary structure which in turn was replaced in 1990 by the new station seen here. The 1910 roof awning has, however, survived and can be seen under the new footbridge. *Authors' Collection/LW*

GENERAL (3): What a wealth of detail there is to be seen in this picture, taken in June 1958, of the entrance to the ex-GWR station at Oxford. On the left is the bridge over Botley Road and on the right the entrance to the ex-LNWR goods depot.

The scene was recreated in March 1991 from the same spot on the roof of the old Frank Coopers marmalade factory. We will leave the reader to compare the two. *J. D. Edwards/LW*

GENERAL (4): The wooden construction of the old station can be clearly seen as 'Modified Hall' No 7912 *Little Linford Hall* arrives at Oxford in June 1964 with the 10.08 am service from York to Bournemouth West.

On Monday 17 March 1992 there's quite a change in the architecture and the motive power to be seen as HST No 43014 arrives with the 8.24 am through service from Stockport to Poole. *S. Boorne/LW*

1
South
Way out
43014

GENERAL (5): 'Castle' No 5071 *Spitfire* stands at Binsey sidings (Cripley Road) on 11 September 1960 with the stock of the 6.55 pm service to Wolverhampton. In the down bay a two-car DMU waits to leave for Bletchley.

The construction of the new station in 1971 saw these sidings lifted and replaced by a new access road to the now defunct refuelling point. Today the area is mainly used for car parking. *M. Mensing/AD*

GENERAL (6): The ex-GW station at Oxford is situated between two bridges. To the south, as already seen, is Botley Road bridge and to the north the Sheepwash Channel bridge which is pictured here on 19 January 1966 as ex-LMS Class '5' No 44875 leaves with a service from Bournemouth to York. On the left is the entrance to the locomotive depot and Station North signal box.

Twenty-five years later, in June 1991, Class '47' No 47823 leaves with the Poole-Manchester service. Note that the bridge has been rebuilt, and also that the 'Abbey Road' sign on the adjacent house has disappeared. *Dr G. Smith/LW*

GENERAL (7): Roughly the same scene looking northwards from the end of the down platform in 1962. From left to right can be seen the ex-Great Western engine shed, opened in 1850, closed to steam in 1965 and demolished during 1968. In the centre is the ex-LNWR engine shed (see page 78), opened in 1851, closed in 1950 and demolished in 1963. On the far right is Oxford Station North signal box, opened in 1900, closed in 1973 and removed in 1974. The tower of St Barnabas Church, seen behind the box, was constructed in 1871.

This is the rather empty-looking scene today. Multiple-aspect signalling was introduced at Oxford on 18 December 1973 after which date all manual signal boxes and signals were removed. Notice that even St Barnabas church tower has been altered. *Both LW*

Authorised Staff
only may use
this crossing
OX
72

OXFORD GWR SHED: The first standard gauge engine shed at Oxford was built by the West Midland Railway at Cripley Meadow in 1854. This single-road depot was extended by the Great Western into a four-road shed in 1862, and this building, which was constructed of wood, survived almost intact until it was demolished in 1968. Towards the end of its life the engine shed yard at Oxford became very tatty and overgrown, as can be seen in this 1962 picture of a line of withdrawn locomotives (two 'Castles' and three 'Halls') standing in the summer sun. In the left background is the ex-LNWR engine shed and on the right the small lifting shop; note the water tank incorporated into the roof.

The area is even more overgrown today. The small refuelling plant that replaced the old steam depot closed some years ago and today stock is only occasionally stabled here. The main reference point is the old lifting shop water tank, sadly since demolished. *W. Turner/LW*

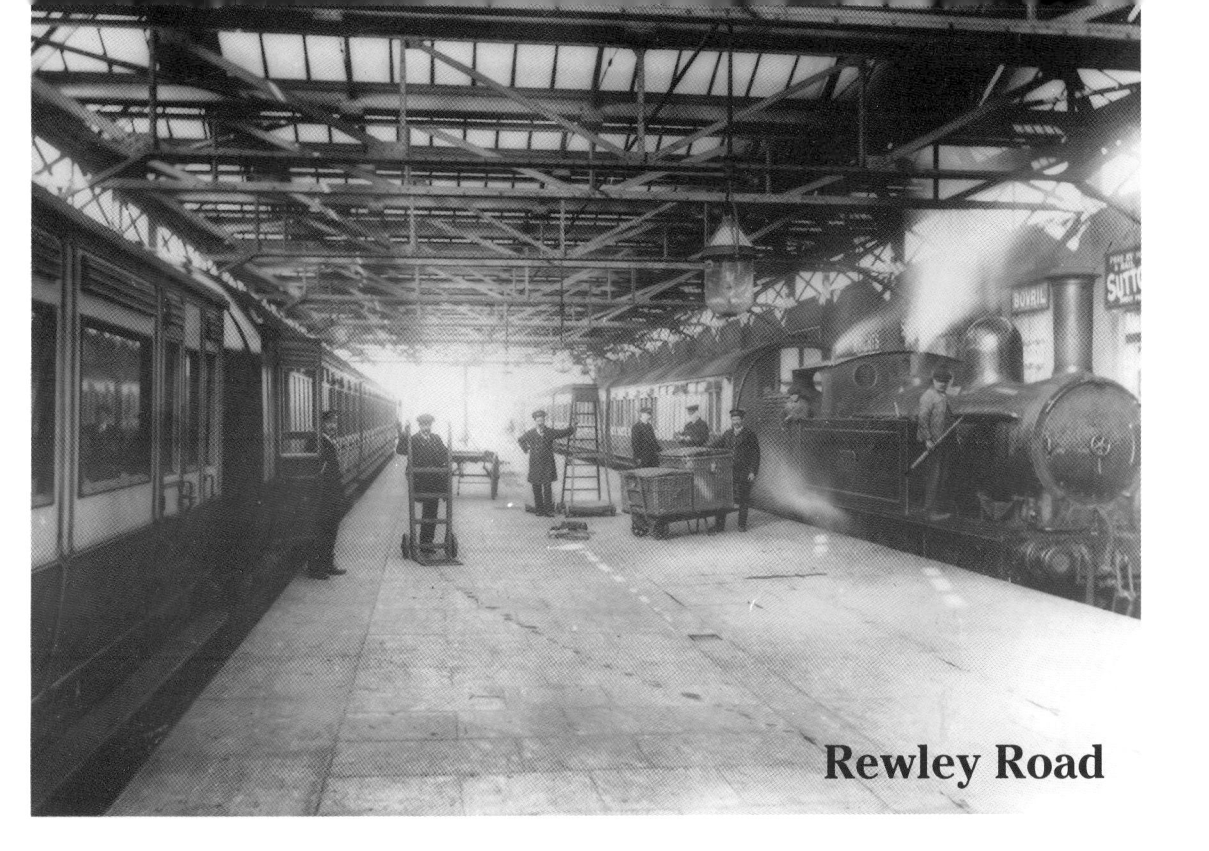

Rewley Road

The London & North Western Railway under the auspices of the Buckinghamshire Railway Company opened its line from Bletchley to Oxford Rewley Road on 20 May 1851. A feature of the station was the unique construction using the same Paxton-designed girder structure that had been used for the Crystal Palace. Passenger services were withdrawn from Rewley Road on 2 October 1951 and from this date services to Bletchley ran to Oxford General. Passenger services to Bletchley were finally withdrawn on 1 January 1968. The line, however, remained open for freight traffic and in May 1987 passenger services were restored once again between Oxford and Bicester by the newly formed Network SouthEast.

REWLEY ROAD (1): The picture above shows the interior of Rewley Road around the turn of the century with LNWR 2-6-2T No 413 standing at platform 2 after arriving from Bletchley.

What remains of the station is now used as a tyre depot. The historic girder structure is now listed; note also in the foreground the original platform paving slabs still in situ. *Authors' Collection/LW*

LONDON MIDLAND & SCOTTISH RAILWAY

BERNARD T
FROST

REWLEY ROAD (2): The following three pictures of Rewley Road were all taken from the top of the old Frank Coopers Marmalade factory. The first, dated 1940 (*above left*) shows the station almost as built.

After closure in 1951 it was used for a while as a railwaymen's hostel. In the 1959 picture (*left*) the entrance awning has been removed and the train shed roof is looking the worse for wear. Bernard T. Frost's coal merchants is still in situ, though.

The third shot (*above*) was taken in March 1991 and shows the station in its present guise as a tyre depot. The coal yards are gone, and the whole area now awaits redevelopment. *BR/J. D. Edwards/LW*

REWLEY ROAD (3): The station entrance on the corner of Hythe Bridge Street is seen in the 1920s. The marmalade factory from where the previous three pictures were taken is on the left.

Standing on the same corner in February 1992, apart from the motor vehicles and the road layout it's amazing how little else has changed. All of the buildings in the previous picture are still in situ and the old marmalade factory is now an antiques centre. *Authors' Collection/LW*

REWLEY ROAD (4): Ex-Midland Railway 4-4-0 No 40551 leaves Rewley Road on 28 September 1951 with the 5.20 pm service to Bedford.

After the station was closed in 1951 the goods yard continued to be used, serving several local coal merchants and a stone yard, but was closed on 5 March 1984 with the remaining track being removed during March 1985. Today the whole area is used for car parking. *Oxford University Railway Society Collection/LW*

REWLEY ROAD (5): The last passenger service to Bletchley leaves Rewley Road on 1 October 1951 hauled by Stanier 2-6-4T No 42667.

Looking from approximately the same spot the remains of the station building can be clearly seen, as can the top of the old Frank Cooper 'Oxford' marmalade factory on the right. *R. Bowen/LW*

REWLEY ROAD (6): The yard at Rewley Road was controlled by the signal box on the left, which was opened in 1883 and closed on 31 July 1959. Immediately beyond the box is the famous swingbridge over the Sheepwash Channel. The ex-Great Western box at Oxford Station North, opened in 1900 and closed on 29 October 1973 (see pages 67-9), can also be clearly seen in this 1958 shot.

The area is now overgrown but the swingbridge (centre background), which is now left permanently open, is a listed structure. *J. D. Edwards/LW*

REWLEY ROAD SHED: The ex-LNWR engine shed at Rewley Road is seen here in 1958. This sub-depot of Bletchley was opened as a three-road through shed in 1851, then was rebuilt as a two-road single-ended shed in 1883. It closed on 3 December 1950, after which date engines were serviced at the adjacent ex-Great Western depot.The water tank and shed building were removed during 1962-3.

The reference point in the second picture is the old up line which is now just a long siding that terminates just north of the swingbridge. *J. D. Edwards/LW*

North from Oxford

OXFORD NORTH JUNCTION: Ex-Midland Railway 0-6-0 No 43529 crosses over to the Bletchley line at Oxford North Junction with the 5.18 pm service to Bedford on 27 September 1954. Bletchley line services ran to and from the ex-Great Western station after the closure of Rewley Road in October 1951.

HST No 43068 passes the same spot on 19 March 1992 with the 11.17 am service from Poole to Glasgow. *Dr G. D. Parks/LW*

ARISTOTLE LANE (1): A little further north, and still looking south, we see Class '40' No D341 approaching Aristotle Lane on 5 June 1965 with a Bletchley line freight. The Western Region line to Banbury and Birmingham is on the right. This section of the old LNWR route into Oxford closed on 29 October 1973 when the new junction at Oxford North was opened (see opposite).

On 19 March 1992 'Sprinter' No 156409 passes the redundant trackbed with the 12.35 pm service to Great Malvern. *AD/LW*

ARISTOTLE LANE (2): Looking north from the bridge at Aristotle Lane on 1 March 1965 we see 2-6-2T No 6126 on the ex-LNWR line arriving with the daily goods service from Bicester Ordnance depot to Hinksey.

On 19 March 1992 No 47147 leaves the Bletchley line at the new Oxford North Junction with the Calvert-Avon rubbish empties. *AD/LW*

Oxford to Bicester

OXFORD ROAD JUNCTION photographed from the adjacent A423 roadbridge in 1958, and looking towards Oxford. Prior to the construction of a bridge in 1935 the road crossed the line on the level here, and the remains of the crossing can be seen on the right. In 1956 the original signal box was replaced by the new structure seen in this photograph. The line diverging away to the right (the Yarnton Loop) was opened in 1854 and gave the Oxford, Worcester & Wolverhampton Railway from Kingham a direct connection via Yarnton and Banbury Road junctions to the Buckinghamshire Railway; up until 1861 through trains were run from Wolverhampton and Worcester to the LNWR terminus at Euston.

The loop was closed and the junction removed in 1966 and today, looking down from the same spot, the changes are obvious as two-car DMU set No L211 passes the site of the old box with a Reading to Bicester London Road service. In the background is the new A34 dual carriageway that connects Oxford with the new M40 motorway extension to Birmingham. *J. D. Edwards/AD*

YARNTON LOOP: Standard Class '4' No 75013 approaches the Woodstock Road crossing on the Yarnton loop on 2 June 1962 with the Yarnton sidings to Bletchley coal empties.

Part of the embankment still survives but the main reference point is the small brick viaduct on the left taking the line over the Oxford Canal. *G. Smith/AD*

YARNTON JUNCTION: At the Yarnton end, 2-6-2T No 6126 leaves the 'Cotswold line' (see page 105ff) and enters the loop with an LCGB Berks and Oxon branch line special on 15 August 1965. Yarnton signal box can just be seen in the left background.

The trackbed of the old loop can be seen on the right in this 7 May 1992 view of the same location. The small concrete bunker see on the left of the older picture can also just be made out behind the electric cable notice.
H. Ballantyne/LW

ISLIP: Back on the Bicester line proper, this is small station at Islip in the 1950s. It was closed in 1968 and removed during the same year.

As already mentioned, passenger services were reinstated by Network SouthEast between Oxford and Bicester in May 1987 and it was not long before the expanding community at Islip wanted their own station, the new Islip, which was built on the site of the old station and opened on 13 May 1989. In this 1991 shot two-car DMU No L850 leaves Islip with the 10.30 am service from Reading to Bicester. *Authors' Collection/AD*

BICESTER LONDON ROAD: This old postcard print shows Bicester London Road probably around the turn of the century. Opened in 1850, the station buildings were constructed of stone; in the centre left alongside the level crossing is the Station Master's house, and on the right is the crossing signal box.

London Road was closed to passenger traffic on 1 January 1968 but was reopened by Network SouthEast in May 1987. However, as can be seen from this picture, taken on 8 March 1992, only basic facilities now remain. The old down platform has gone, as has the signal box, while the crossing gates are now operated from the platform by loco crews travelling through to Calvert and Wolverton. Looking at the state of the old up buildings one wonders for just how much longer they will survive. *Authors' Collection/LW*

BICESTER NORTH (1): Bicester's other station, Bicester North, is situated on the ex-GWR 'cut-off' route from Paddington to Birmingham and was opened on 1 July 1910. Here, on 31 May 1960, No 4907 *Broughton Hall*, on the 4.34 pm Paddington-Wolverhampton semi-fast service, waits to pick up a slip coach from the 5.10 pm fast service to Birmingham.

Although the line has been singled between Princes Risborough and Aynho Junction, both platforms at Bicester North have recently been modernised. On Sunday 8 March 1992 Network 'Turbo' No 165013 prepares to depart with the 10.50 am service to Marylebone. *M. Mensing/LW*

BICESTER NORTH (1): A second sequence taken from the up platform on 25 August 1960 shows No 5994 *Roydon Hall*, also on the 4.34 pm Paddington-Wolverhampton service, collecting the slip coach. The Bicester slip was the last slip coach working in the country, finally coming to an end on 9 September 1960.

In the 1992 picture the refurbished platform and footbridge can clearly be seen - compare also the track layout with the previous picture. *M. Mensing/LW*

WOLVERCOT PLATFORM: We now return to the main line northwards from Oxford, but this time looking at the former Great Western side of the layout. The Great Western opened number of railmotor halts in the Oxford area on 1 February 1908, and one of these was situated just north of Oxford at Wolvercot; here we see it from the adjacent roadbridge in around 1911. The railmotor is probably *en route* to Heyford. The halt, which was renamed Wolvercot Platform in 1910, probably to avoid confusion with the nearby LNWR Halt, was closed in 1915.

In March 1991 there is no trace of Wolvercot Platform although the track layout doesn't appear to have changed much. The lake on the left, seen in the older shot, is now partially hidden by the trees. *Authors' Collection/LW*

WOLVERCOTE JUNCTION: A short distance northwards from the previous picture is Wolvercote Junction. Here, on a glorious Saturday 2 June 1962, No 7013 *Bristol Castle* runs off the 'Cotswold line' with the up 'Cathedrals Express'.

Wolvercote Junction signal box was closed on 14 October 1973 and the junction is now controlled by the Oxford panel. On Tuesday 3 March 1992 'Sprinter' No 156402 crosses the junction with the 12.13 pm service from Great Malvern. *Dr G. Smith/LW*

Fairford branch

The Witney Railway was opened on 14 November 1861. This 8-mile branch connected with the Oxford, Worcester & Wolverhampton route approximately 3 miles north of Oxford at Yarnton. On 15 January 1873 the line was extended by the East Gloucestershire Railway Company through to Fairford. Passenger services were withdrawn on 18 June 1962, although the original Witney Railway section remained open for goods services until 2 November 1970.

YARNTON JUNCTION (1) was opened on 14 November 1861, and is seen above in the 1930s - note the ornate shelter on the down platform and the ivy-covered Station Master's house on the right. In the centre is the ex-Oxford, Worcester & Wolverhampton Railway route to Worcester and diverging away to the left is the Fairford branch.

Yarnton Junction was closed on 18 June 1962 and today all that remains is the 'Cotswold line' to Worcester which was singled between Wolvercote Junction and Kingham on 29 November 1971. *Authors' Collection/AD*

YARNTON JUNCTION (2) looking towards Oxford on 19 May 1962 as 'Castle' No 7036 *Lydford Castle* rushes through with the 9.15 am Paddington-Hereford service. The signal box here was built especially high to afford the signalman a good view of both junctions, and was closed on 28 March 1971.

The same location on 7 May 1992 shows 'Sprinter' No 150105 on the 12.13 pm Great Malvern-Oxford service. *Both LW*

YARNTON JUNCTION (3): During the Second World War a number of new sidings together with a turntable were installed at Yarnton. The sidings were used for goods traffic that ran direct from Cambridge and Bletchley to Worcester and beyond, and the entrance to them can be seen on the right of this picture, which also shows 'Hall' No 6948 *Holbrooke Hall* passing through in August 1959 with a down service to Worcester.

The same spot in 1992 is identified by the concrete sand bunker and also the piece of rail that once supported a 'Beware of the Trains' notice at the end of the down platform. The sidings were taken out of use on 6 July 1966 but the turntable pit survived for many years after closure. The whole area to the south of the line is now being used for gravel extraction. *J. D. Edwards/AD*

CASSINGTON HALT: This was the first station along the branch; 0-6-0 No 2221 arrives with the 4.24 pm service from Oxford to Fairford in June 1960. A halt platform which stood on the south side of the single line was opened here on 9 March 1936, but construction of the new A40 road to Witney saw the halt moved to a new site to the east of the new roadbridge and north of the line.

Today the trackbed has been concreted over to form a new access road serving the various sand extraction sites in the area. *J. D. Edwards/LW*

EYNSHAM was opened on 14 November 1861. Originally a single-platform station, a new concrete platform (on the left of the photo) was added in August 1944. Passenger traffic was withdrawn on 18 June 1962 but Eynsham remained open for goods until 26 April 1965. Note the large goods shed - this was used for a number of years after the station closed for building theatre sets, but was demolished in 1987.

The second photo shows the same spot today. The trackbed now forms a service road into the giant Oxford Instruments complex. The wartime platform was removed by the Great Western Society in 1984 and has now been reassembled at Didcot Railway Centre, while the notice from the signal box door now hangs in LW's study! *Authors' Collection/LW*

SOUTH LEIGH, pictured here in around 1959, consisted of a single platform and a small wooden booking office that probably dated from the opening of the station in 1861 (compare it with the original station building at Witney on the opposite page). A level crossing stood at the Oxford end of the station, and the siding in the background served the Second World War food store in the centre of the picture.

Today a house, aptly named South Leigh Station, has been constructed over the trackbed, but the old food store building, although long closed, still remains. *Authors' Collection/LW*

WITNEY (1): This is all that remains of the original terminus at Witney, pictured in the early 1960s. The station was opened by the Witney Railway Company on 14 November 1861 and closed to passengers on 15 January 1873.

Today the site is still used by Marriotts, the local coal merchant, and in this 7 April 1992 picture several of the buildings remain in situ. The original station building, however, is quite safe, having been dismantled and moved to Wallingford where one hopes it will see further use. *AD/LW*

WITNEY (2) was the main station on the branch, and this is the 'new' station which was opened on 15 January 1873 when the Witney Railway was extended by the East Gloucestershire Company through to Fairford. Taken from alongside the signal box on the up platform, it shows 0-6-0 No 3653 taking water after arriving with the 4.26 pm service from Oxford on 11 June 1962.

Unfortunately there is now no obvious reference point, so you will have to take our word for it that this is the same location! The only clue is that the area is now designated the 'Station Industrial Estate'. *H. Ballantyne/LW*

BRIZE NORTON AND BAMPTON was a small but busy station, and is pictured here in May 1959. It was situated alongside the Brize Norton airfield and was opened as Bampton (Oxon) in 1873, being enlarged (note the extension to the platform) and renamed Brize Norton and Bampton on 1 May 1940.

Due to MOD security this second shot was the only one that we could obtain. It is taken from the small road-bridge that crosses the old trackbed and shows the large warehouse complex that has now completely obliterated the site. *Authors' Collection/LW*

CARTERTON was the next station along the line, pictured here on 2 June 1953 as 0-6-0PT No 7411 arrives with the 4.18 pm service from Oxford to Fairford. Carterton was opened on 10 August 1944 in order to deal with the increase in service traffic to the nearby airfield, and was actually closer to the village of Black Bourton than Carterton.

Today only the roadbridge identifies the site; the trackbed leads to a farm and the road across the bridge terminates at the airfield fence. *H. Ballantyne/LW*

ALVESCOT station, looking down from the adjacent road bridge. On the platform is a typical East Gloucestershire Railway stone station building and a Great Western 'pagoda' waiting room. A single siding served a coal yard.

The same spot today, and what a mess! There is still a coal yard here but the cutting is also full of scrap and the underside of the roadbridge is now used to store bales of hay. *Authors' Collection/LW*

3653

LECHLADE was just over the border in Gloucestershire. On 11 June 1962 0-6-0T No 3653 arrives with the 4.26 pm service from Oxford (*above left*).

The second picture (*left*) was taken some five years after closure in 1967 and shows the station still basically intact. Note that the field in the top left has now become a gravel pit.

By July 1978 (*top*) all trace of the old station has gone, although the coal yard remains. The gravel pit is now a lake. The final shot (*above*) shows Lechlade in January 1991. Nature has finally taken control. *AD/LW*

FAIRFORD (1): This was the end of the line, pictured here in the 1950s with 0-6-0 pannier tank No 7411 preparing to leave with a service to Oxford. Note the early type of GWR milepost (89) at the bottom right of the photograph.

A large industrial estate now covers the station area but the old stone station building (centre) still survives. *Real Photos/AD*

FAIRFORD (2): At the very end of the line, just beyond the station, was the engine shed and turntable. On 22 March 1962 0-6-0T No 3653 is turned after arriving with the 12.18 pm service from Oxford. The loco depot closed with the rest of the line on 18 June 1962.

Although filled in, the outline of the turntable pit is still clearly visible in this picture taken in January 1991. *Both AD*

'Cotswold Line'

The Oxford, Worcester & Wolverhampton Railway opened its line from Wolverhampton to Oxford in 1853. This 89-mile-long route reached Oxford by way of a junction some 3 miles north of Oxford at Wolvercote (see page 90). During the late 1960s and early '70s the 'Cotswold Line', as it became known, was in imminent danger of closure, but with the support of the then local area manager, a degree of rationalisation and the formation of the Cotswold Line Promotion Group, the line was saved. This one-time main line is today under the jurisdiction of BR's 'Regional Railways'.

HANDBOROUGH Station around the turn of the century. Originally known as Handborough Junction when the OW&WR operated its service from Worcester to Euston in 1854, here trains would connect with the GWR via Wolvercote Junction and Oxford. The station even had a small refreshment room. Handborough came to public notice in 1965 when Winston Churchill was buried at nearby Bladon, his funeral train running to Handborough.

Today Handborough is designated a halt. Only the up platform remains, as does the Station Master's house, now a private dwelling. The Oxford Bus Preservation Trust has its headquarters in the old goods yard. *Authors' Collection/AD*

COMBE HALT: 'Castle' No 7004 *Eastnor Castle* runs through the down platform at Combe Halt in July 1961 with a Paddington to Worcester service. The halt was opened on 8 July 1935, the up and down platforms being staggered. Note the small roadbridge and milepost 71.

Today (*centre right*) the track has now been singled and the down platform removed. The roadbridge has also been rebuilt, but milepost 71 can just be seen by the wire fence.

The third picture (*right*) shows Combe Halt today. The single wooden platform is situated on the up side at milepost 71.44. *Rev Hughes/AD/AD*

KINGHAM (1): 'Chipping Norton Junction' as it then was is pictured here in 1906. A '517' Class 0-4-2T is waiting in the branch platform on the left, possibly on a service to Cheltenham, while another member of the same class can be seen under the bridge. Chipping Norton Junction was renamed Kingham in 1909.

The branch platforms are now derelict and the attractive station buildings have been replaced by a modern flat-roofed structure (right). 'Sprinter' No 155311 departs with the 10.44 am service from Great Malvern to Oxford. *Authors' Collection/LW*

KINGHAM (2): The 5.50 pm service from Cheltenham St James hauled by 2-6-2T No 6126 crosses over the OW&WR route to Worcester as it arrives at Kingham on 2 September 1961. The line to Cheltenham diverges away to the left, the Chipping Norton line to the right.The large water tank stood alongside the small single-road engine shed which is obscured in this picture by the engine.

Today only the Cotswold line remains. The embankment of the 'direct line' which joined the Cheltenham and Chipping Norton routes, crossing the Cotswold line by a bridge, can just be seen on the left background. *M. Mensing/LW*

Oxford to Aynho

KIDLINGTON (1): Returning once more to the main line north of Oxford, but now taking the main Banbury route, the first station was Kidlington. It was opened in January 1855 as Langford Lane, was renamed Woodstock Road in July of the same year, and Kidlington on 19 May 1890. In this 1930s shot (*above left*) 'County' 4-4-0 No 3806 *County Kildare* waits with a stopping service to Banbury, whilst in the bay with the branch service to Woodstock is '517' Class 0-4-2T No 1473 *Fair Rosamund*.

Kidlington Station closed on 2 November 1964. In this early 1970s shot (*left*) little remains of the platforms but the down-side building is more or less intact. The yard was used at this time for motor vehicle repairs.

The third shot (*above*) shows the same scene today; the site is now part of the Station Industrial Estate. In 1991 the old station building burned down - its remains can just be seen in the centre of the picture. Luckily the old Station Master's house (left) still remains. *Authors' Collection/S. Boorne/AD*

Woodstock branch

The 3-mile Woodstock branch was opened on 19 May 1890, running from Kidlington to the small Oxfordshire town of Woodstock, famous for Blenheim Palace, the home of the Marlborough family and birthplace of Winston Churchill; in fact, for the whole of its existence the station sign at Woodstock read 'Blenheim for Woodstock'. The branch was closed completely on Monday 1 March 1954.

SHIPTON ON CHERWELL (1) was the only intermediate station on the branch, and is pictured above shortly before closure as a group of enthusiasts await the arrival of a train.

The second picture (*above right*) shows the same location in around 1959.

Today (*right*) the site is overgrown, but the remains of the wooden platform are still in situ, albeit covered by undergrowth. *Authors' Collection/J. Edwards/AD*

SHIPTON ON CHERWELL (2): The entrance to the halt stood adjacent the main A423 Banbury Road - the large sign was certainly meant to encourage travel by rail!

In 1992 only the abutments of the bridge remain. Note that the signpost beyond has been changed and the trees have gone. With the opening of the new M40 extension the road has now been downgraded. *Authors' Collection/AD*

WOODSTOCK (1): These two views of the station frontage were taken in 1958 and 1991 respectively. The latter shot clearly illustrates the way that the original building has been incorporated into a garage complex (see overleaf). What is even more remarkable is the way that the owner has retained many of the original station signs within what is now part of the workshop. *Lens of Sutton/LW*

BLENHEIM &
WOODSTOCK

GENTLEMEN

WOODSTOCK (2): The interior of the small terminus is pictured here (*above left*) in the 1920s. The running-in board proclaims 'Blenheim for Woodstock', a throwback to the opening of the line when much of the money was provided by the then Duke of Marlborough.

After closure (*left*) the station remained derelict but intact, and is seen here in around 1959.

In the 1960s the site was purchased by Young's Garage. The old garage, glimpsed beyond the station buildings in the 1959 view, was moved from across the road and on to the station site. The remaining part of the station yard was sold to Blakes of Didcot who constructed a small housing estate.

The final picture in this sequence (*above*) shows the yard at the back of the garage; note that the platform awning together with some of the station's topiary is still visible on the left. *Authors' Collection/J. Edwards/LW*

KIDLINGTON (2): Back on the main line and looking north from the A423 roadbridge at Kidlington in August 1962, 'Castle' No 5076 *Gladiator* passes Kidlington signal box with the 8.42 am Shrewsbury to Paddington parcels. On the left between the siding and the down main is the track of the by now closed Woodstock branch, used at this time as a goods avoiding line.

Kidlington box closed on 14 September 1968, and the down loop and siding were removed during the same year. On 16 April 1992 Class '58' No 58048 *Coventry Colliery* approaches the roadbridge with a MGR service to Didcot. *S. Boorne/LW*

SHIPTON ON CHERWELL CEMENT WORKS (1): Just north of Kidlington was a small industrial system serving the large cement works at Shipton on Cherwell.The works were opened in 1929 and closed in 1989, although cement production had ceased some years previously. Several small engines were employed over the years to bring the limestone up from the nearby quarry.

In this first picture, taken on 9 March 1969, three of these stand at the coaling point: left to right they are Robert Stephenson & Hawthorn No 7742, William Bagnall No 2178, and Andrew Barclay No 2041. A small engine shed was provided some distance away alongside the main line.

On 20 March 1992 the works are derelict and the site of the coaling area is now identified by the lamp-post on the left and large building on the right. *AD/LW*

SHIPTON ON CHERWELL CEMENT WORKS (2): From the quarry to the processing plant, trains had to climb quite a steep gradient. In this shot Andrew Barclay No 2041 is seen hard at work pushing its train-load of limestone up from the quarry.

Although the quarry has closed and the tracks have gone, the small weighbridge hut in the background remains as does the girder structure of the overhead conveyor. At the time of writing there is talk of infilling the quarry with rubbish which will be brought to the site by rail. *AD/LW*

BLETCHINGTON was opened as Woodstock Road in May 1851; it was renamed Kirtlington in July 1855 and Bletchington on 11 August 1890. The Shipton on Cherwell cement works just visited can be seen under the bridge.

Passenger services were withdrawn from Bletchington on 2 November 1964. The building remained in situ for a while but was removed in around 1970. The cement works, although now closed, still form a backdrop to this winter 1991 shot. Today the old goods yard at Bletchington is still in use as a coal yard. *J. D. Edwards/LW*

HEYFORD: Here the railway runs alongside the Oxford Canal for a short distance. The first picture shows the station in the 1920s; the small signal box on the down platform was opened around 1880, and was closed on 16 September 1968.

The station underwent some rationalisation in the late 1960s when the up platform buildings were removed. The down side building lasted until the mid-1980s when it was dismantled by members of the Great Western Society and taken to Didcot Railway Centre. The result is that the canal basin can now be seen as HST No 43074 rushes through the recently refurbished station with a Derby to Poole service on Saturday 22 February 1992. *Authors' Collection/AD*

AYNHO FOR DEDDINGTON: Aynho was opened on 2 September 1850 by the Oxford & Rugby Railway Company. In the left background of this 1955 view is the flyover carrying the down line of the 1910 'cut-off' route over the tracks to join the Oxford line at Aynho Junction. A small halt called Aynho Park was situated on the 'new' line.

Aynho for Deddington was closed to passengers on 2 November 1964 (Aynho Park had been closed on 7 January 1963). The up building was soon removed, but the down building was used for a number of years by the local coal merchant. All that remains of it, pictured here in March 1992, is now listed and at the time of writing is up for sale. The signal box was closed on 16 September 1968. *GW Trust/AD*

AYNHO JUNCTION: Ex-Great Western 2-6-2T No 4176 leaves the 'cut-off' route at Aynho Junction on 29 August 1962 with a limestone train from Ardley to Harbury (Greaves Sidings).

During April 1992 the manual box at Aynho Junction was taken out and all the semaphores removed. On 16 April the closed box awaits its fate as Class '47' No 47844 *The Derby and Derbyshire Chamber of Commerce and Industry* runs past the junction with the 09.18 Brighton-Glasgow service. *M. Mensing/LW*

AYNHO WATER TROUGHS: Situated just north of the junction were Aynho water troughs, pictured here on 29 August 1962 as 'Castle' No 5019 *Treago Castle* runs through with the 4.15 pm Paddington-Bicester-Banbury semi-fast service.

A new 'Chiltern Line' turbo, No 165038, passes the same spot on 16 April 1992. Note the trout lakes in the field on the left. *M. Mensing/LW*

Banbury and Cheltenham Direct line

The Banbury & Cheltenham Direct Railway opened on 6 April 1887. This cross-country route left the Banbury to Oxford main line at Kings Sutton and ran via Chipping Norton and Kingham through to Cheltenham. Passenger services were withdrawn between Banbury and Chipping Norton on 4 June 1951, from Kingham to Cheltenham on 15 October 1962 and between Chipping Norton and Kingham on 3 December 1962.

KINGS SUTTON: A Great Western 2-2-2 runs into King Sutton at around the turn of the century with a service for Oxford (*above*). The station which was opened in 1872 was of an unusual design - note the rather ornate brickwork and chimney stacks on the up-side building. Sadly this did not survive and was removed during the 1960s - why was it never listed? However, the small shelter on the down platform is still in situ.

Today Kings Sutton is served by Network SouthEast 'Chiltern Line' and 'Thames Line' services. One of the large running-in boards from the old station can be seen displayed on the side of a nearby barn. *Authors' Collection/AD*

ADDERBURY was the first station on the line after leaving Kings Sutton. This 1920s shot was taken from the nearby Banbury Road and shows a '517' Class 0-4-2T on a Banbury-Kingham service.

Adderbury was closed to passengers on 4 June 1951 but remained open for goods until 4 December 1967, after which the station site was used for many years by a local seed merchant. Various warehouses now cover the area, the only reference point to the 1920s shot being the old station road on the left that still gives access to the site. *Authors' Collection/LW*

BLOXHAM (1): This lovely picture of Bloxham was taken in 1925 by the late Frank Packer of Chipping Norton and shows Station Master Lloyd and his family together with other members of his staff.

Fifty-six years later the scene is one of desolation. Only the roadbridge gives reference to the first picture. *Packer Collection/LW*

BLOXHAM (2): We just had to include this second picture of Bloxham which was taken from the roadbridge on the same day. It shows the wonderful station garden complete with 'Bloxham GWR' picked out in stones (right). It was a time when 'pride in the job' had some meaning.

Looking down from the bridge in 1991, I'm sure your comments would be the same as ours - unprintable! *Packer Collection/LW*

HOOK NORTON: Another Frank Packer photograph shows Hook Norton in 1925. The small signal box can been seen on the down platform, and the building on the left is the Railway Hotel.

Today the site is almost inaccessible. Fighting my way through the undergrowth I was able to photograph the trackbed, and found that the down platform is still in situ 'buried' under the bushes on the left. The only reference point between the two pictures is the distant hill. The old station hotel is still standing and is today a private residence. *Packer Collection/LW*

CHIPPING NORTON (1): As already mentioned, Chipping Norton became the terminus of the line from Kingham for passengers in January 1951. Here, on 2 April 1955, Gloucester-allocated 2-6-2T No 5538 stands at the station with the Saturdays only 4.35 pm service to Kingham.

Today the site has become an industrial estate, the station area being used by a builders merchant. The road bridge, now filled in, is the reference point. *H. Ballantyne/LW*

CHIPPING NORTON (2): Looking in the opposite direction from the previous view, 4-4-0 No 9015 leaves for Banbury with the SLS South Midlander enthusiasts' special on 24 April 1955.

The cutting and tunnel, the latter now bricked up, can now only be photographed from the old road bridge. *H. Ballantyne/LW*

SARSDEN HALT was opened on 2 July 1906, and was actually situated almost 2 miles from Sarsden village. This photograph shows the halt in the early 1920s. The adjacent level crossing, which led down to Sarsden Mill, and the single siding were controlled from the small signal box.

The trackbed here, which stands on the Churchill estate, can be easily traced. The chalet bungalow on the left is built almost on the site of the old crossing and is aptly named 'Sarsden Halt'. The main reference point between the two photographs is the old mill on the right, now converted into a house. *Packer Collection/LW*

Banbury

The Great Western, under the auspices of the Oxford & Rugby Railway, reached Banbury on 2 September 1850 via a single broad gauge line that ran from Millstream Junction, Oxford. By 1852 the Rugby section had been dropped and during the same year the line was doubled and opened through to Birmingham by the Birmingham & Oxford Railway Company.

BANBURY GENERAL: The station at Banbury was mostly constructed of wood (*above left*). It was designed by Richard Pauling with an overall roof in the Brunel style and survived almost unchanged for over 100 years, but had fallen into a poor state of repair when this picture was taken on 25 July 1949.

During 1952 the overall roof was removed and new platform awnings were constructed (*below left*). Note also that the footbridge was covered.

Between 1956 and 1958, under the BR Modernisation Plan, the old station was demolished and replaced with the concrete and brick structure pictured here (*above*). The fourth view, from the adjacent roadbridge (*below*), shows to good effect the north end of the station as Class '47' No 47809 *Finsbury Park* prepares to depart with a Paddington-Liverpool service in the summer of 1991. *BR(3)/LW*

BANBURY GW ENGINE SHED: The Great Western opened its new engine shed at Banbury on 29 September 1908, to replace a small single-road shed that stood adjacent to the station. The new four-road shed had an allocation of between 40 and 50 engines, mostly freight types.In September 1963 Banbury was transferred to Midland Region control. In this picture, taken on 13 June 1965, the Midland influence has prevailed, as only two ex-Great Western locomotives can be seen. The shed was closed to steam in October 1966 but continued to be used for stabling diesels for a short time.

The site today is derelict and covered with rubbish. Large trenches have been ploughed out near the entrance to stop travellers setting up camp, although walking through the undergrowth it is still possible to find some of the shed foundations. *M. Soden/LW*

BANBURY YARD (1): Ex-Great Western 2-8-0 No 2853 leaves Banbury Yard with an up goods in March 1962. The yards at Banbury once extended for nearly a mile and had a capacity of over 2,000 wagons. Note the Station Master's house on the right of the picture.

Today the once large yard at Banbury comprises just a few sidings which are now used mainly for storage purposes. In September 1990 an unidentified Class '47' leaves for Reading with an up engineering train. The Station Master's house has now been demolished and replaced by the large office complex seen on the right. *A. Simpkins/LW*

Merton Street

The LNWR under the auspices of the Buckinghamshire Railway Company opened its station at Banbury Merton Street on 1 May 1850.

MERTON STREET (1): This picture of the station (*above*) was taken in 1958 and shows not only the neat and tidy frontage but also the excellent condition of the station at this time. It is worth comparing its design to that provided by the same company just one year later at Oxford (pages 72-3). The circular building on the left background is the Banbury livestock market, one of the largest in the country.

During 1957 services to Buckingham and Bletchley were taken over by single-car DMUs but passenger services were withdrawn on 31 December 1960. Goods services lasted until 1963 and the site was cleared during 1966. *J. D. Edwards/LW*

MERTON STREET (2): On 6 August 1960 railcars M79900 and M79901 wait to leave with the 3.45 pm service to Buckingham. Apart from the removal of the glazed roof the station is almost intact - note especially the low platform.

The second photo, taken in March 1991, shows the station site today; one of the tracks can still just be made out under the parked trailers. *M. Mensing/LW*

MERTON STREET (3): Looking in the other direction from the previous view, single car DMU No M79900 arrives on 25 August 1960 with the 12.30 pm service from Bletchley.

The gas holder provides the reference point for the contrasting April 1992 shot. *M. Mensing/LW*

BANBURY YARD (2): Pictured from the waterworks road bridge, just north of Banbury (GW), is Standard Class '9F' 2-10-0 No 92004 as it runs into the large goods yard in July 1964 with a coal train from the Midlands. The connection with the Great Central line at Banbury Junction is just obscured by the signal on the left.

On 16 April 1992 Class '58' No 58028 passes the same spot with a Coalville-Didcot MGR working. The old cold store on the right, built during the Second World War, is still in use. *M. Soden/LW*

NORTH FROM BANBURY: Looking south back towards the station, 'Castle' No 5076 *Gladiator* is seen accelerating away from Banbury in 1963 with a summer extra from the South Coast to the Midlands.

Yes, this is the same spot! New housing has been built on the site of the old yard, but the most obvious change is the new northern relief road which crosses the railway at this point and now dominates the whole scene. The HST is on a Poole-Glasgow service. *M. Soden/LW*

MFI

INDEX OF LOCATIONS